Whirlagust 3

The Yaffle Prize 2021

© Copyright the authors 2022

Published by Yaffle Press, 2022

https://www.yafflepress.co.uk/

All rights reserved. No part of this book may be copied, reproduced, stored in a retrieval system or transmitted, in any form or by any electronic or mechanical means without the prior permission of the copyright holder.

ISBN:	978-1-913122-30-0
Cover design:	Lorna Faye Dunsire
Typesetting:	Mike Farren
Editing:	Mark Connors and Gill Lambert
Administration:	Mike Farren

Introduction: Whirlagust 3

The best-laid plans of everyone have gone astray over the last couple of years. As we noted in the previous Yaffle Prize anthology, our publication plans had taken a hit because of the impact of COVID on live performances and the difficulty and uncertainty of launching new books in the circumstances.

We had also planned to make the Yaffle Prize an annual event but because of the difficulty of coming together and the necessity to catch up with ourselves, we find that we're launching our third competition anthology well into our fourth year.

However, the extra time that we have taken over this has meant that we had a record level of entries, with over 440 poems submitted by more than 150 poets from the UK, USA, Europe and elsewhere.

Though quantity is no guarantee of quality, we were again impressed and humbled by the standard of the submissions. We could easily have produced a much longer anthology and still included many more remarkable poems. The high standard, however, made our job in selecting the shortlist and winners more difficult than ever – so difficult that we had to call in a guest judge. Many thanks to Sharon Larkin for helping us with those tricky decisions.

As ever, it's great to see some of our choices vindicated by the fact that we've selected work by established, acknowledged poets with a strong track record behind them. However, what is even more exciting is the discovery of distinctive, vital new voices from whom we can expect so much more. Look out for some of these voices represented in Yaffle collections and pamphlets in the near future.

Contents

First Prize
One of my nine lives stayed in
    Venezuela — *Sue Burge* — 1

Second Prize
The Leeds Mummy visits Meanwood
    Park — *Ian Harker* — 3

Third Prize
Chav — *Holly Bars* — 5

Highly Commended
Baby steps — *Oz Hardwick* — 6
Oh Karen — *Sharon Phillips* — 7

Commended
After My Sister Leaves — *Rachel Davies* — 8
Caesarean — *Pauline Rowe* — 9
Dressmaking — *Diane Cockburn* — 10
Round — *Christopher M. James* — 11
A Woman Like That — *Jennifer A. McGowan* — 13

Long-Listed
The angler — *Nicola Carter* — 14
Apology — *Rachel Glass* — 15
Bathing in a Trafalgar Square
    Fountain — *Jo Brandon* — 17
Between the Rowan and the Birch, a
    Doorway to the New World — *Maggie Mackay* — 18
Bloodworm — *Abigail Rowland* — 19
Body in the Underworld — *Becky Cherriman* — 20
Box set death march — *Lucy Heuschen* — 21
Brodgar — *Andy Humphrey* — 22
Builder's Mate — *Laura Strickland* — 23
By the tide of Humber — *John Foggin* — 24
Colour Theory — *Laura Strickland* — 25

Days that followed	– Deborah A Lyons	26
The dead pornstars	– Ian Harker	27
Death of a Dog	– Tonnie Richmond	28
Don't Mind Us	– Charles G Lauder Jr	29
The Dress	– Wendy-Jane Walton	31
Dressmaking	– Sue Mackrell	32
Frida Kahlo	– Kathleen Strafford	33
He was a midfield dynamo	– Simon Tindale	34
Hear the lonesome locomotive roll	– John Irving Clarke	35
A House by the Sea	– Michał Choiński	37
I sat next to Christina	– Kathleen Strafford	38
I scratch words in the dusk	– Katy Mahon	40
In a Body	– Jennifer A. McGowan	41
Lie in	– Bev Morris	42
Life's rotten shabby trick	– Pat Simmons	43
Listening to the Leeds Library	– T.P. O'Connor	44
Lockdown Love Poem, April 2020	– Andy Humphrey	45
Me, But Happy	– Rachel Glass	46
The Milkmaid	– Frances Thomas	47
The Names of Trees	– Andy Humphrey	48
Pomegranate Seeds	– Frances Thomas	50
The Real Venus	– Katy Mahon	51
Redundancy	– Roger Hare	52
Remembering all the small shops	– John Foggin	53
Rescuing the Giraffe	– Sue Finch	54
Reunion	– Lucy Dixcart	56
The Science of Ghosts	– Kathy Gee	57
Slack Water Level	– Sue Butler	58
Something Lost	– Clare Wigzell	59
Staying Home	– Sheila Jacob	60
Swimming with Dolphins	– Jenny Robb	62
These are fleeting thoughts	– Tina Cole	63
What we Learn from Stones	– Tina Cole	65
Why We Stopped	– Michał Choiński	66

Yaffle Team and judge
The Wife's Lament	– *Gill Lambert*	67
Propagating a treasure trove	– *Lorna Faye Dunsire*	68
Asking for it	– *Mike Farren*	70
Closing Day	– *Mark Connors*	72
You Knit	– *Sharon Larkin*	73

First Prize

One of my nine lives stayed in Venezuela

I didn't know death could be the colour of sunshine
the swaying mule I rode through the Andes to this cable car station
now seems a miracle of stability
hindsight a tumour swelling in a seethe of *if onlys*
I look across at Merida   we have slithered 6km of the 12 & now hang
strung & still
an almost perfect mid-way point

I decide who to jettison   first on my list the two builders who boarded
with a steel lintel they threaded through the car's open windows
the safety notice obscured by its bulk
a child stops crying as if he's read my mind
we are packed in   noisy guests in a party kitchen
a daily power-cut is normal here although there appears to be so much
energy
heat thick as a coat and an afternoon breeze I'd normally welcome

I think back to the three-day weeks of my childhood   no streetlights
candles & calor-gas
the boozy smell of uncollected rubbish   I long for firm cold dirty
streets
enough of this pretty   bougainvillea butterflies fuschia paint on
adobe
I wonder if we'll see the flight to Caracas pass   the steward smiling
and beckoning
pointing to my empty seat
I won't miss the men on street corners carrying machetes

First Prize

                        one of the builders coughs   stubs out his roll-up
the car judders   resumes its slow descent & I too am slow to come back
                                              to life   to give a weary cheer
                            I guess death is always a kind of suspension
      just the long release of a breath you've been holding for a lifetime

Sue Burge

Second Prize
The Leeds Mummy visits Meanwood Park

The Leeds Mummy abandons his chariot in the fumes and tailbacks
of Meanwood Road and yomps it to the park accompanied
by goldfinches and red kites, the beck like a handrail taking him
from the monks' bridge to the tannery where Meanwood's skin
is pulled inside-out, where we are drowned in warm vats
under the healthy smell of horses and under the Iron Age grace
of the heron. Nesyamun ducks into ancient woodland.
The quarry is a stone bird bath in which blackbirds
hold themselves still in the cold. Magpies and crows tip water
into the wells of themselves. Jays saw into the branches
with acorns in their beaks. These are the holy places—
water and bridges over water, stone roaring over the weir,
a pair of egrets like hieroglyphs while the dog-headed gods
go for a walk along the Meanwood Valley Trail.
The woods bubble green and blue.
There are names carved into the trees.
There are dates carved into the rock. The wood is alive
and the rocks are alive. A Pharaoh cums into the Nile.
Thoth throws hawthorn into the beck. Nesyamun doubles back
past Meanwood Colony with its residents in white against a wire fence,
past the ruins of Scotland Mill where Matthew Murray
is broken on his own wheel, past the Beckett Home
where the children float in the air held up by misregistered red
        balloons.
There used to be tram lines and they rumble under the tarmac.
There used to be overhead wires and they fizz and spark above our
        heads.
The whole city is sparking—the road is rumbling end to end.
And on the monks' bridge a Pharaoh throws white and green into the
        water.

Second Prize

O let the beck come back
O let the Nile recede with its tail between its legs
O let the beck leave green and hawthorn and the smell
of horses
everyone inside their cold gold head
with hawthorn and the smell of water

Ian Harker

Third Prize

Chav

Something about it being another redundant Sunday, the feel of wind nipping my cheeks, walking down my street with houses the same council-red brick as my old estate and hoarding the same deranged litter, sets a shadow of my younger self in front of me.

And then I'm wearing the burberry pink scarf I bought from Rosie Pounds for two-ninety-nine, the slouch boots and denim cropped jacket I nicked from my sister. I hear the bite of my words as I lair the streets in the centre of an arm link with two other girls. I can feel the tack of my lip-gloss I got free in a magazine, the sky with the same hooker-blue of my eyeshadow, tarmac the kohl of my eyeliner, two twiddles of hair gelled to my face which stay unfettered, like the ponytail I've whipped to a messy bun.

And then my bun tightens and tidies, and I'm wearing my first school uniform, blue jumper/grey skirt/blue shirt, with a PVC apron. I'm coating my fingers in PVA and peeling it off. I'm painting with a palette of colours that stink of rust. I'm crying after swallowing apple seeds, shouting at Lisa Baker she can't have my second-best teddy when I die. I'm telling Sarah Hall to *be quiet! We are playing Universities, and you have to be quiet in university.* She's Cambridge, I'm Oxford.

And then I step out of it, back into the body of my grown self, into my mute coloured coat, earthy mum-tones, and into my life, the one that has gotten so quiet. I walk home, unlock the door, look at the dishes. I scrub, waiting for my ten-year-old to come home from his dad's, try to work out how I'm going to afford to get a degree. And I wonder how much of who I was I still am, who I could've been if I'd have lived anywhere else, who my son will become.

Holly Bars

Highly Commended

Baby Steps

Brush the frost from the mirror, the sleep from your eyes. It's gone midsummer and you're way behind the curve, watching the year kick up dust in the dry distance, while here you are, still shuffling in your winter dressing gown, clutching unsent Christmas cards and Valentines, your millionth pot of coffee percolating in the kitchen. You know in your bones that it's time you left the nest, but the twigs you gathered with such textbook love have grown through your flesh, and you can't tell which hanks of wool are bedding and which are your own. In the last newspaper that arrived, each crossword clue leads to a different word for snow, even as the pages yellow and flutter, impatient to be folded into a simple boat, or merely to rest across your face on a gritty south coast strand. So, shear the shaggy pelt from your almost human skin, wipe away everything that clings to cold. Midsummer's already sleeping, though the cock's crowing in a far-off barn. Put away your winter moods. Nail the wardrobe shut.

Oz Hardwick

Highly Commended
Oh Karen

what if you'd been
on channel five tonight

not swamped
by pastel flounces
flimsy skin stretched
over jutting bones
smile racking
your mouth

nor crooning
on a Vegas stage
hair teased
to a froth of platinum
botox congealing
your brow

but in a black singlet
grey hair close-cropped
tattoos sprawling
on taut bronze biceps
pounding
your drum kit

as if you'd never
been stopped

Sharon Phillips
(for Karen Carpenter, 1950-1983)

Commended

After My Sister Leaves

I roll our history into a poster tube, hide it
in the orange crates behind the boy scout hut,

For years I've felt her tongue hard and flat
as a spatula, now I'm free. No more

love thy sister. I've put an end to her
gratuitous rudeness. I skip over turnstiles,

a froghopper giddy with effort to recall
what I've chosen to forget. So now

I can please myself. I'll take an ice pick
to the build-up of frost in my chest.

I have other sisters. We'll meet
in the Hubba Hubba, clink glasses

of Monkeywrench on the rocks, say
y'know what?

Rachel Davies

Commended

Caesarean

In Roman times the mothers didn't live.

The Registrar said "risk of fatal bleed"
assessed me as a dud for natural birth.
I thought of misappropriated names.

The surgeon came to see me on the ward,
suggested that he cut my tubes as well.
We fought about it and he washed his hands.
They sliced and clamped me open for the sixth.

What's the significant organ here? And risks?

Shamed by the student's silence,
afraid of sepsis and the threat of wounds,
I called out: "bladder" and they laughed.
"There's a first" he said,

as though my abdomen were dentate
and could speak.

Pauline Rowe

Commended

Dressmaking

This was the spell tucked into the flow of stitches from her old sewing
 machine:
'Always anchor nine seeds into the hem of every garment.'

With each needle pierce the scent of night owl bled
into the scullery and scuttled behind the kitchen cabinet.

Luna moth eggs hidden in the seams sang;
sometimes we could hear their green chirrup,

feathering the dirty dishes;
sometimes her voice quivered the air like the coddle of an egg.

The town didn't understand Mother;
we didn't understand her either;   we only watched.

We drank her broth, and no one asked what was in it:
her world was a canyon of strange.

She never unpicked her work;
she sewed her own life.

Diane Cockburn

Commended
Round

Those days before child abuse...
>I was let out

to deliver thousands and read none,
>though the swing of gates

sighed daily for scant news
>of the living. Every spring,

the half-light of a crenellated skyline,
>fortresses hiding in suburbs,

their decoy names beside doors:
>*Chez nous, Bon repos, Xanadu...*

In winter, the streetlamp beams
>wrapped scarce early risers

into the mist, one curt existence
>after another. And I,

stealthy in each season, for the sake
>of the dogs, their folly

and their fear of ghosts. I learnt
>the numbers, followed them

like at Sunday school, fathoming
>how to come close, how

to disappear, burying silence in steps,
>internalising the world.

Commended

None of *them* ever changed,
        not for another gospel,

not even at tinselled Christmas.
        Unbroken linearity

called *round* when done.
        It felt round as I pedalled home,

when streets rustled like branches.
        Sometimes, my chain skipped.

Christopher M. James

Commended

A Woman Like That
"A woman like that is not afraid to die." – A. Sexton

Even as she lies in the sterile bed with a tube
running out of her mouth, the nurses ask questions
and she, stubborn, responds in sign, unstoppable.

She's spent her life giving out, not giving up.
Sandwiches. Advice. Sex. Warm clothes.
Putting female sanitary products in food bank boxes.

She knew the tyranny of blood, the fear of it,
as she edged down the hallway with a wad in her pants
knowing her gait, her dashes to the toilet,
gave her away. She turned fourteen and learned

to say Fuck all of it. She partied in the streets,
slept in tunnels every protest until
the police baton found her head. She is that kind
of woman. Minx. Maven. Gamine. Bolshevik.

The nurses all wish they were her.

Jennifer A. McGowan

The angler

So you thought you could lure me close
with those lashes casting shadows on your cheek,
hiding eyes that change with the weather.
Oh deceptive fisher boy with your deep desires,
feathery flames in dark water.

I am hooked and drawn by the long lines of the mind,
netted by strong arms.
Sinuous skin and iridescent strikes of light and I am gone.
Released and whipping fins through the wave.

You know sometimes you'll find me
hugging the muddy floor of self-deprecation,
sometimes free flying from the bubbling surface,
sometimes in between.
And you will choose your cast accordingly.

Nicola Carter

Apology
after Caroline Bird

I don't know when the fish started dying
but the scientists can't explain this guilty phenomenon.
I don't know when illegal flowers started blooming
from goldfish gills, choking them from the inside out.
But no one could hide the belly-up whales
and narwhals and manta rays.

The conspiracy theorists say *of course*
the government is behind it all.
I wish it were true.

I was too distracted by his charm
and compliments to notice any of this,
too trapped in his ocean blue eyes.
I drive past the dead fish flowers piled high
on the side of the road, thought unlucky,
thought a curse.

You noticed. Of course you did.
It's hard to miss the whale carcass in your front garden.
And no matter how many explosives the scientists
put in the whale's mouth
or my heart, nothing can move it
and you were covered in remains months ago.
You can't get rid of the smell.

I know why he chose you: no arguments,
only jokes, always happiness.
Always happiness.

He would've chosen you if you lived an ocean away
and all the fish would've survived that kind of love.
You're lucky like that, I guess.

Just between us, I wish I'd met you before him.
I could've loved you like he does.
I could've loved you better.
The birds would've stopped flying because of our love.

Rachel Glass

Bathing in a Trafalgar Square Fountain
after Susanna and the Elders

I've blocked phone signals, all cameras jammed,
you can record in your mind's eye – this is still a public space
but you can't zoom-in, play-me-back, stupid-face-pause –
this moment belongs to me.
You can jump in too but don't even think about letting your leg,
or anything else, bump mine. If you want to splash, make noise,
I don't mind, don't want to take the bustle out of life –
just the hassle, the heckle.

I'm leaving clothes out to warm on the Lion's paws,
I'll save my blushes for Sir Edwin's formal busts
while my breasts goosepimple in bus-fumed air,
while pigeons gather about my shoulders like epaulettes
and my bare ass is all the power-pose I need.

Later, others slide off high-waisted trousers and slit-back skirts,
look me in the eye, nod and talk as our bodies are gently water-swayed.
When the day clocks-out and we feel sun-fade shivers quake our
        bodies,
like old alone-at-night fears, we help one another with arm-twisting
        zips
and cloth-covered buttons, walk back towards the tube, journey —
        alight.

Jo Brandon

Between the Rowan and the Birch, a Doorway to the New World

She is a stray branch of their rowan, berry-fat
on the edge of the longhouse gable,
her grandfather's planting against evil.

She is the stray branch of a family tree,
stretching for generations, undisturbed gravestones,
dishevelled stones, witness to burning.

She stretches out through manitou and raindrops
to strangers, their unfamiliar ways becoming habit,
skies wider than old skies, until old ways go,

half-remembered, rowan, shining birchwood
pruned to the length of songs, dances,
random letters tucked in dressing table drawers.

Maggie Mackay

Bloodworm

Winter fishing. I bait my hook. Not every business
    can be pretty.
        Not every fish will

imitate the dancing tench or Our Blessed Lady of
    the Rock and Stream, the iridescent
        lipstick-painted grayling.

The monstrous, though, have no less need
    for regard. The ugly are no less
        deserving - see

my carp and bream, the fearsome barbel,
    my bony-headed, slant-toothed
        pike.

Such predators stir silted depths
    where corpses have been known to beckon
        grasping hooks with

fleshless fingers. There is history
    in fishing in December, an element of exposure.
        Cold,

invited in, will inhabit the bones.
    Many fish   will move slowly   slowly
        to the bait.

Abigail Rowland

Body in the Underworld

Each time we go in, we descend
below the earth. Who are we looking for
in the liquid dark but our lost wives?

We have swum too close to the sand martins' nests.
The banks are littered
with microplastics, parabens and tinny speakers.

Weren't we among the leaves when I let go your hand?
A snake made for the other shore. I looked back
and you were gone.

This edge tree has grown listening,
records eddies in its bark
that swell to ripples of feeling.

If I can only get the stroke right,
I'll find the chord to you.
Under kingfisher wing? In minnow cascade?

My limbs know the way.
Their metre sings
with diction of cold
and the undercurrent
This – where trust is.

Becky Cherriman

Box set death march[1]

starting from
what box set to watch tonight

stopping at
whose turn it is for the kids

diverted around
why we never f*ck anymore

Lucy Heuschen

---

[1] *I wish I had coined this phrase! But credit belongs to the writers of the awesome HBO series Succession, which inspired this poem.*

Brodgar

It is not in sky
but in stone,
the memory of us:

in the plunge of broken stars,
the long drowning, then breaking
the surface, birth;

in the cracking of hillsides,
the needle ice, the ceaseless
chiselling;

and in the circle, the locking
of stone into stone, the melding
into mist and wind and silence.

Andy Humphrey

Builder's Mate

In those days, the radio announced
which schools were closed for snow.
No Facebook posts from the mother
who knows everything.
Just a voice reading names out
in the glow of a three-bar fire.

That day, I went to work with my dad.
While he built a wall, I smoothed
the snow into a perfect slide.
Swapping my wellies for shoes
that had just the right type of sole
I ran, arms outstretched
through the rush of air,
then up the hill to do it again.

I'd hold his trowel while he cupped
his hands round a cigarette.
I'd press a brick on top of another and hold
the spirit level until the green bubble rested.
He handed me a Mars Bar from his pocket.

Later, when the sun fell in and the cars lit up
like fairy lights on our Christmas tree,
we'd trudge home, through snow turning
to sludge, feel the grit on our cheeks,
his rough hand in mine.

Laura Strickland

By the tide of Humber

Here's the brick I fetched
from the grit of a beach so hot
my feet were blistered,

that day at Spurn where sometimes
clouds of goldcrest blown off-course
make landfall, exhausted, too weak to move,
are picked off by rats and gulls.

This brick, more pig-iron than clay,
a small cylinder block. Small pebbles
wedged in four of its six holes,

picked up the day two dolphins came
rollercoasting up the muddy Humber
while container ships sat top-heavy
on the tightrope horizon, waiting for the tide.

Brittle marram, dusty thrift, rusted beer cans,
bits of glass at the end of the walked world.
Two dolphins, distant as birds
and blithe as birds. This brick.

John Foggin

Colour Theory

When I wanted yellow sweets,
I learned to lose my temper
when she brought me red ones.
When I found out that *Ginger*
was not my dad's name,
I learned that nicknames stick
when you forget who you are.
When I bought purple fishnets
in Leeds with the older girls,
I learned how to be edgy.
When I dyed my hair black
before my Maths exam,
and got caught in the rain,
I learned that ratio
could not balance me.
When I saw russet feathers
floating after the fox got in,
I learned that silence follows death.
But when I shared an orange
with my girlfriend, when the pith
peeled away and the juice
smeared our mouths,

I learned how to pan for gold.

Laura Strickland

Days that followed

When he walked out and left,
know that he stole a part of you.
No point in trying to pull it back,

call after it or trace its path.
A lawyer can't help, nor the police,
for the part of you was freely given.

You didn't think that when he took it,
there'd be a wound, red and livid,
which would take too long to heal,

and as life ticks on, putting a foot
before the other, propelling forward blindly;
you'll wade through hours and days.

People will still open windows,
wash the dishes and do the crossword
but you'll look on, like it's a movie,

stand lost in the teeming life
around you, like a speeded up film
of Times Square or Piccadilly.

You won't die, though briefly you'll want to.
Slowly there'll be an awakening,
a sure groping towards connection

when despite what's behind you,
you'll re-fill the bird feeder, plant bulbs
and glance across a Friday-night bar.

Deborah A Lyons

The dead pornstars

The joke's on us: we're the ones
who are dying. We'll never match
how warm they are -

the dead pornstars are full of colour
and bodyweight, they are covered
in cave paintings and clouds,

they're stickmen with heat flaring
inside them, infrared footage
of a lava flow - each second,

each scene. The dead pornstars
keep going long after we've logged off,
moaning from the bottom of a well

into a bright circle of sky
with us peering down at them.
They make us feel so flat,

like so much lack, backlit
beneath us and their skin
shining in a long arc.

Ian Harker

Death of a Dog
For Mary Anning (1799 - 1847)

That day, that cold, wet, winter's day,
when the cliff crumbled and killed your little dog
and nearly killed you, did you curse them,
those well-heeled comfortable clergymen and squires,
with time on their hands and their scientific societies,
gentlemen's clubs and easy lives,
who bought your Ichthyosaur, your Plesiosaurus,
and all your other other fossils
for a pittance and forget to mention
how you, a poor working woman, struggled and laboured
to provide for their success?
Did you curse them that day? Dinosaurs.

Tonnie Richmond

Don't Mind Us

After Hurricane Katrina and in the midst of recovery,
of FEMA trailers parked on the lawns and driveways of homes
whose sides, if still standing, were exposed like a doll's house,
they came in busloads to tour the destruction
of New Orleans' Ninth Ward, where Bobby Rae
hacked his way onto his roof from the attic,
and Mrs Peters lay down on her bed to wait,
hearing what she believed to be the levees exploding,
a sacrifice of her neighborhood to save the rest of the city.
Such a popular spot on the route, the buses would pause
on the fringe for panoramic photos and videos,
though the black residents asked them not to stop,
to keep moving, to not make a buck off their suffering.

How different were we, seven of us packed behind
the tinted windows of Papaw's plush-carpeted van
swivelling in our chairs as he pointed out the highlights
of his old stomping grounds—West Houston Street
where he grew up, Brackenridge Park for fishing
and first dates with Mamaw, that corner the site
of a bowling alley and his job as a pin boy—
then the second half along the east side of town, never
the quickest way back home, where everything was dingy
and miserable and black, the regaled childhood tales stopped,
replaced by clicking tongues, shaking heads,
and in a loud whisper from Mom or MaMaw,
the story of PaPaw's Uncle John, stabbed
by a black man while trying to break up a fight.

I feared us breaking down, yet wondered what it was like
to live there, while others came and went at leisure,
as if moving through a border crossing.

Charles G. Lauder, Jr.

The Dress

I found it when we cleared her wardrobe,
after Granny's death.
I never saw her wear it, she had kept it
hanging there for more than sixty years.
She sewed it for herself as a young bride,
same age as you are now,
my mother said, *in 1921,*
silk velvet sourced especially from London.

A shifting sheen of russet and of oxblood,
some patchy fading where the nap's worn down,
a heart shaped neckline,
mirrored in the V shaped waist
with five self-covered buttons ranked in pride,
a tie sash at the back, two simple poppers,
full skirt flares out from fitted hips,
to drape quite modestly below the knee.

I slip it on and mother pops me in.
My waist's the same — but smaller chest,
leaves bodice fabric spare in draping folds,
the sash when tied lends curves I don't possess.
I face the mirror, flounce and turn,
become young Edith with her handsome Tom.

A party for the family; my older cousin stared.
He said *I love your dress,* and I explained
how it was Granny's.
He told me *You should wear it often.*
His gaze made me uncomfortable.
I never did again.

Wendy-Jane Walton

Dressmaking

Swathes of fabric laid over the table - velvet, corduroy, crisp new
    cotton.
I loved her sureness, a swift rip, sharp cut, neat pattern of pinking
    shears,
pins in mouth, frown of concentration (right side inside, make sure
    pattern matches,)
sucking the end of Sylko thread, drawing it through the
black lacquered sewing machine, electric speed of the treadle,
then tedium of hem-pinning (Stand on the table. Keep still. Stop
    fidgeting.)

The clothes she made for me are there in photographs,
blue dungarees for first steps, rosebud bridesmaid's dress
itchy tartan skirt, gingham school-dress.

At thirteen I spurned home-made clothes,
wanted Mary Quant mini-skirts, wide belts,
white patterned tights and ribbed polo necks.

At fourteen I followed her coffin wearing a black dress
    she hadn't made.

Sue Mackrell

Frida Kahlo

Her fused brows   a bird's fanned feathers
            flapping to take flight
            its claws digging into her skin

She rages against New York's fat cats
hates the Hoi Polloi
Adores Dr Couney's infant sideshow
            yearns to feel their tiny movements
            thinks incubators might be her answer
            for caesareans that never arrive

Miscarriage after miscarriage
she paints all of her violent bloody stillbirths
even a midwife's view
of her own limp head emerging from her mother

The tram's handrail severed her heart from her spine
& her womb from her pelvis influencing revenge
portraits of her stormy stubborn face
        leafless twig veins
           thorns choking her blood-stained neck
                & whispering petals of roses

Tired of being a childless woman
Frida dresses in men's clothes
        chops off dark strands
        becomes her own Delilah
Affairs of unruly hair
        becomes her epitaph littering her yellow chair and floor
            like dead sperm or black seaweed snakes
            she drowns in curls and infidelity

Kathleen Strafford

He was a midfield dynamo

with a left foot
to die for
who left us for dead
on his way
to the bar,
a deceptive turn,
a drop of the shoulder,
to line up a shot,
put it away.
So talented,
it was a crime
he slept through
the Spurs trial.
Some youths
get wasted
too young.
Two years later
a small club bought him
for a pint
when the window closed
and he'd stopped eating.
'Watch this,' he'd say
kicking empties
into a skip,
'Sweet as a nut
in a crack jar.'

Simon Tindale

Hear the lonesome locomotive roll

Like the low moan of an idling loco pitching in crescendo.

Our luggage stowed,
by duty-bound porters
we have been *sirred* and *ma'amed*
and polished into place

until we spin through the dark on Amtrak
from Freedom Gateway Detroit
to the city of 'scrapers, pizzas
and Al Capone's Valentine's rout.

We scroll through a corner of Michigan,
skim Indiana and roll into Illinois
where each shack and patch of real estate
is tolled by a bell from effects.

It's the game we play,
everyone here is from central casting
that man in the suit
may well be a spy.

Sitting across from Cagney
we joke about matinee stardom
until dirty rat that I am,
I need to go and freshen.

Misreading the restroom signage, I wait
and practise a look of fellow feeling,
dipping into my English pool of protocol,
aren't these things just sent to try us?

Hearing the lock slide open, seeing the
changing colour of the figure displayed,
I prepare to share my smile
and reflect our mutual plight.

But eye contact with the black girl is slight,
drawing from *her* centuries-old well of destiny,
she stiffens, then shrinks, from the white guy,
the one *she* has made to wait.

The baggage we carry
which is ours by rite,
the long track we follow
and the hill we climb.

Like a storm about to break across a brooding lake.

John Irving Clarke

A House by the Sea

Right after they remarried,
Grześ and Judy moved to Parszczyce,
and began to fantasize
about dying there.
They imagined buying a shared sepulchre,
close to their new house,
and leaving their fortune
to an orang-utan rescue fund in Borneo.
Over dinners they enjoyed speculating
of who'd fly over to attend their funerals.
They began exchanging keepsakes –
photos of each other,
styled to make them look old.
Every day, they felt more like mannequins
moved by acts of will,
framed only by the context.
They'd hide from each other
that they checked each other's clothes
for the signs of decay.
Finally, the only asset they shared
was the fear of remaining in possession
of those things they had.

Michał Choiński

I Sat Next to Christina
Most remembered poetry workshop

What's in the box?
she said *I call him Yum*
her smile could get me through winter
she was a Shaman witch
enchanted with four letter words
        conjuring love potions
        embracing her pet snake
        gracing a coyote with last rites

I wasn't surprised
when her mouse escaped
jumping onto the floor
we all shrieked scrambling
        onto tables or chairs
        as it scurried up inside
        Christina's pant leg

With clinical coolness
she unbuckled
        unsnapped
               unzipped
held onto her panties
slid her tight jeans down
to retrieve her snake's next meal
plopping it back in its box.

Oh how uncanny a lesson
when desire and need
become the same animal
    to seize the moment
      break the rules
strip it all down   expose yourself
      but keep a modest mystery
      searching & swinging
          that last line
              by its tail

Kathleen Strafford

I scratch words in the dusk

In this half-light I know
that memory is a form of seeing.
It's fallible still, remoteness
thrumming at the edges
of recollection; a photo

revealing both absence
of an object and the shape of things
distorted: a rubber ball, a mooring ring,
the causes of my trip and fall
towards the edge

where sun-baked concrete
met water, where the *meltemi*
had chased brown limbs
along Naoussa harbour,
freedom lapping at hemline and nape.

My father saved my life that day,
his grip-reaction knife-sharp.
In his grasp, my sandalled feet swung up
towards the noon.

Katy Mahon

In a Body

The seat belt sign goes off
                and the middle-aged women
surge to the toilets in a body

crack necks
                raise on tiptoes
smile their eyes over masks

at each other and the stewardess
                who has an inkling what they're going through
how bodies mutate

thicken
                acquire new urgencies
habits they'd love to break but instead

suck a lozenge
                suck their teeth
disinfect the seat before sitting

and wink at the stewardess who knows

Jennifer A. McGowan

Lie in

a groaning yawn as the weekend crests and falls into Sunday, fingernails on my eardrums, ice in my spine, necrotic hope settling in my heart

he's awake, blood moving faster with every stretch, time slows to a cobweb shivering in the early morning breeze insistent through the stained cardboard curtains, I stick to its threads, a ladybird with one wing trapped open

belching out yesterday, inhaling my air in a greedy gulp, he steadies his decline

    tablet, tablet, tablet

      swallow

lying rabbit-still, instinct betrays me: I breathe

his pounce is swift and certain for an old fox; he bites my slender, white throat, softer than the cherry blossom petals cavorting with late spring snow, falling in a deadly embrace to the stinking carpet

I yield

  thirty-year habit

  noticing pigeons at dusk

  iridescent rats

Bev Morris

Life's rotten shabby trick
Gloucester Cathedral: memorial to Mrs Elizabeth Williams, died in childbirth aged 17

It's the alabaster bow that breaks your heart,
neatly signing off a life never begun,
stone baby stone-swaddled, staring blind
up from its chrism shroud.

After nine months together these two
should have met, been snuggled close.
They do not touch; her hand
clasps a prayer book.

Did their eyes meet briefly? Did she notice
its dimpled chin, so like her own?
Its smile is mysterious, unconnected.
She stares unseeing across the nave.

Death has clothed her decorously
in fold upon fold of decency,
covered the torn and fevered flesh,
closed her legs.

Pat Simmons

Listening to the Leeds Library

A soft thunk as a book returns to its shelf,
a kaleidoscope of voices through an open window,
the precise punctuation as a door closes.

Flute and bassoon converse at the Issue Desk,
a metronomic foot taps out a tempo,
a pensive andante, sotto voce.

Rich in flowers, Bookcase 43 chirrups and hums,
bright young volumes chatter to their dozing elders,
the stairs creak like a barque under sail.

Someone coughs, tea trickles into a cup.
The air lies heavy as a billion words murmur,
patiently waiting for their turn to speak.

T.P. O'Connor

Lockdown Love Poem, April 2020

Five years ago today I wrote a poem
inside your birthday card. Bought you craft gin.
Tickets for your favourite author. Took you
for a vintage railway carriage
afternoon tea. Music. We held hands.

Today, before you're up, I wash the dishes.
Check my breathing, cough into the crook
of my elbow. Disinfect the post.
I hand over your birthday cards, then switch
over the radio. Tune out the news:

masks, statistics, PPE. What I want
for your birthday this year is to keep you
safe. To drop you off at school each day.
To listen as you talk detentions, marking –
the ordinary punctuation of our life.

Let me make you a negroni, sit with you
through movie afternoons in black and white
(tuxedo, ballgown, dancing cheek to cheek).
I check my breathing. Cough into my sleeve.
Wait out the sunlight's journey round the room.

Andy Humphrey

Me, But Happy
after Neil Hilborn

Let me tell you that the sun was still glowing
even after you left, after I stopped opening
the curtains, when I opened the curtains again.

I started going to my therapist again. By therapist,
I mean God. I mean God listens better than I listen
to myself. I mean I've started listening to myself again.

This morning, I told my best joke to the pigeon
perched on the roof of my car and she laughed.
I'm laughing again. I realised the lump on the inside

of my lower lip, the one that turns selfies into Picassos,
tastes like strawberries. I'm smiling again. Trust me
when I say I'm the best thing that's ever happened to me.

Rachel Glass

The Milkmaid

Yes sir, come in. Only don't mind if I get on with my work.
What? A pudding, sir, bread pudding – the master likes it and we have
    lots of bread today,
Like we did that day he came.
What? Just as I was – I thought I'd have to sit, or something,
But he said, no just get on with whatever it is you're doing.
Then he stopped me when I was pouring milk, of all things. Yes, do
    that,
Do that again, he said.

He was a strange one, they all said so,
The way he painted, the things he painted,
Me in my old clothes pouring milk.
What? The light? Yes, I keep this table by the window.
He said, about the light that it was good, it was the way he liked it,
The way it falls on stuff, well, it has to, doesn't it, in a kitchen?
But why paint an old brown bowl, when Madam has lovely china
    upstairs?
He just said, he liked the... texture... he said, and the way the light...
    something...
The way the light somethinged on it.

Oh yes, he was an odd one, always broke, they said
Though he had a wife and kids to feed.
You'd think he wouldn't have been so fussy about what he painted,
Madam in her new silk dress that looks so nice,
Or Sir with his gun and his dog...
Not me in the kitchen making a pudding, what for?

Would you like a mug of milk sir? We have good milk here.
Fresh from the cow this morning.

I mean, you can't just paint light, can you?

Frances Thomas

The Names of Trees

Silver birches are easy:
gangly anorexic trunks,
scabbed chalkiness of bark.
You've no trouble with weeping willows.
The bright green riot
of the one at the end of your street
makes you smile every time we pass.

Laburnum is your favourite.
You can't bring yourself
to believe me when I tell you
how those carnival hues
clothe a warning. I point out
others. Larch's mossy teardrops;
yeomanly outlines of oaks.

You tremor with the leaves
in the unseasonal chill,
ask me about elms. Ghost trees,
these, greyed into half-light and history –
and me too young to have known
a countryside before
their sickening.

Afterwards, in the car,
you ask me what God's number is.
I try to tell you
about Planck's constant: the seed
at the heart of creation
that makes planets spin in orbit,
trees branch and leaf.

From the set of your shoulders, it's clear
I haven't convinced you.

Such small things, these:
seeds
and Planck's constant
and cancers
growing into things
neither of us can name.

Andy Humphrey

Pomegranate Seeds

When first she arrived, she simply wept,
Soaked her pillow with tears.
What should I do? I loved her so;
a god's love should be enough.
I found her jewels from the deepest depths,
emeralds, sapphires, opals flashing fire;
Their colours stained the darkness of my walls;
slaves mined silver, wrought curious bracelets;
girls like these things.
But still she wept.
Called for her mother. I am your mother now, I said,
your sister and your brother, you need none but me.
Then she grew hungry, but kept her lips tight shut;
(she knew the score.)
I sent out into her world for them,
Pomegranates, glowing, tawny rose
piled in their bowl like hot coals.
I envied her the tasting;
she held the seeds in her hand, rubies against the dark,
Inhaled their scent, could not hold out.
The juice ran down her chin, stained her fingers.
Six seeds, a month for each.
She must stay with me now.
I am not unkind; give her all she can want.
I can comfort and console,
My touch can be fire, or satin,
Golden couches, heaped jewels, scents in crystal vials,
It is all before her. She need not mind the darkness,
I make it light for her.
A thousand thousand slaves attend her every whim.

And yet she will not love me.

Frances Thomas

The Real Venus

What do you think, Gaspar, when you see me hanging
on your scarlet wall?
Do you sip your tea, hand on chest, lean in
                            and scrutinise me

or do you sit back on your plush chair, let your arms
hang by your sides,
        and gape in awe?

For D. (and you) I turned away, displayed
only curves
which the courteous painter softened
with his brush.

You cannot sink fingers into my bronze hair or touch
                            my flushed cheek;

only gaze at the smudged sweep of my elusive face
          where you must miss
                  a certain meekness
               defied
                       by an elegant posture

of conviction,
or indifference.

Katy Mahon

Redundancy

Domestic hardware is designed
with a timed demise
to subvert desire for repair
when the damn thing breaks – *it's
obsolescence sir, just throw it away.*

My Grandfather worked 'til he boiled to death
in an unsupervised public bathhouse.
He was cleaning away a day spent pouring
molten manganese bronze
into ship propeller molds
housed alongside the Mersey.

I work at staying still: keep my door
shut: let ringing phones
go: practice
lying low – my slightest breath
risk revealing
the secret weeping
of blistered flesh.

Roger Hare

Remembering all the small shops

Whatever happened to them,
the ones that grew in abandoned spots?
Not the house-shops that sold next to nothing,
but the ones that started off
as clinker-sided sheds with felted roofs,
and later with barbed wire on top.

Those sheds that turned up in gaps
like old mill gateways in walls,
or where a house burned down;
the ones that seemed organic,
grew like caddises, and were always
painted green, and maybe there was a factory
somewhere making nothing but this green gloss paint
that couldn't quite keep down the damp
that pushed orange fungus blisters through the cracks.

Those shops that sold cigarettes
to children, five Woodbines
and five matches in a paper bag.
Cheap sweets, cheap pop, papers,
shoelaces and hairnets and combs.

Shops like Alec's, Mucky Jim's.
Their owners cramped as hermit crabs
behind a shiny counter, men (they were always men)
who had lost the way of speech,
took the small change like an insult badly borne.

Did they sleep there?
Where did they go?

John Foggin

Rescuing the Giraffe

Counting the tangled legs, I make it six.
One head so I count again.
This time I make it an almost knotted four
and its eyes are fixed on mine as if I could be its mother.

But how do you retrieve
a giraffe from an earthquake crack?
And then what do you do with it?
The trees are bare
and I feel unqualified for this emergency act.

I am almost sure its skin would feel like suede
and those hot chocolate eyes are imploring me.

You are a poet, you owe me this, it says,
so, I sit on the edge
reach down my hands
pat its gentle rump.

It is all muscle under that thin, soft skin.
I stroke tentatively.
Don't bite me, I say,
and the giraffe is offended.
OK, what I mean is
it might be uncomfortable
while I sort out your legs.

It barely makes a sound as I work.
Released feet scrabble to find their place
on the jagged sides of the hole.
It is ready for the hauling.

My arms cradle its stomach
leaving the legs to dangle
and I have him rising.

He is as unsteady as the day he was born;
skidding like a skater on their first rink.
But finally he is up, shaking off confusion
and I am seeing the size of our shadows.

Sue Finch

Reunion

She's waiting at the porter's lodge
in her flower jeans.
She tuts as I navigate the quad –
my map is full of holes. I think of the first time.
October winds, dead leaf confetti.

A grand piano flanks the bed.
Her face is snow. Crushed by clever underwear,
I ease myself into the dress, inch by inch.
Read all about it: python swallows entire cow.
She laughs angrily.

The bar. She's already there, knocking back shots.
Champagne. I remember the song.
Milk-heavy, spinning away, I land in Hall
beside an old foe, now sporting jowls.
He quizzes me about my job – his is better.

She's rolling her eyes.
Drags me to some former friends. We sift
through weddings, children, work – nothing sticks.
The picture I was before has jigsawed
and all the edges are missing.

Drizzle gleams yellow.
I reclaim my room and plumb myself in.
A metronome keeps time – soundtrack of my life.
Voices rise, subside. I leave before dawn,
tugged by an unseen cord.

Lucy Dixcart

The Science of Ghosts
(after Dr Alan C Smith FInstP, FIET, FRAS)

                                         If they were really real,

        all apparitions would comply   with basic physics.

               Ghosts cannot be vapour   (light is not refracted)

              and there's no reflection   (so they can't be shadows).

             A ghost that is transparent   must be gas but then,

                              what holds   its form together?

       They must be light absorbing   (no bright colours).

and magnetic forces must be feeble   (gasses leak).

                       So that's why sound   can only travel slowly.

                                         That's why all ghosts moan.

Kathy Gee

Slack Water Level

                all along the five rise
                bargehands chunter
                beer belches lay on
                the still evening air
farmhands curse   drive barmpot cows
out the Hoist Wood run off dockhands
drip sweat coal dust dark   quicklime
clouded   embers of the year   drift
down   scatter a top dressing   over
my murky face layer after layer   like
empty cornsacks   tossed away from
the loading bay   white ice spikes
macerate   as I soften rot draw down
bare black tree bones   towpath run to
puddled mud   getting out place green
mossed   silent   no hooves to scour it
grave-black grave-still   I hold secrets
in the slack water levels   no-one asks
me to tell   lumps of gold bags of coin
bit by bit year by year I hide their flash
concrete weights   rusty chains   bones
of bastards   buggers   burglars
                alongside meditators
                mindfulness pedlars
                healthy heart hustlers
                tomorrow happen sun
                power barges happen
                demolition

A slack water level is a slow moving stretch of canal between two locks

Sue Butler

Something Lost

Once we inhaled our village spores,
smelled the first frost, the mud in the lane,
sucked in hairs and pollen in spring,
the mites living in the old gate.
We took in dust in dry summers
the mulch when we tramped the woods.
Carrying baskets up Old Martha's Hill,
we gulped in flies and tiny seeds.
Our noses knew the brackishness of
water after rainless days,
dankness when the river flooded.
We breathed in the morning breeze,
a hint of warmth, tinged with green,
exhaled air for the oak in the yard.

Clare Wigzell

Staying Home
After Carl Tomlinson

I often envy the ones
who wedged their elbows
on bedroom windowsills,
gazed across lines
of wooden-fenced gardens
and never felt the nudge
of unhatched wings
beneath their shoulder blades.

Girls who left school
after O-levels, got engaged
to boys they met at work
and saved for a house
on the new estate,
never ached to breast
the city's rim as sun dipped
beyond the Rotunda.

Girls who stayed, bought
their Mum and Dad's old place,
added a patio, front porch.
They carry travel passes,
don't fumble for the exact fare
or say *To The Glebe, please,*
as though bus drivers remember
every demolished pub.

They organise coffee mornings,
campaign for Christmas lights
above the local shops.
They take their grandkids
to the library's activity hour –
Hallowe'en masks, this week,
then Diwali: paper lanterns,
greeting cards, dancing and song.

Sheila Jacob

Swimming with Dolphins
Bay of Islands, New Zealand, 1996

She came from the deep,
nudged my swollen belly
gently, again and again, as if to say,
Take care, go back.

My nipples, shocked by cold,
ached with a new pain.

I swam to the boat
with her touch in my bones,
her song in my womb.

My bottle-nosed dolphin
forgot to eat, forgot to feed
her young, so busy, following boats,
swimming with people.

Jenny Robb

These are fleeting thoughts

like children who ring the doorbell
and run away. Sitting in the kitchen
I am thinking my world has grown

too small. Two metres, how quickly
that distance has become our lens,
opportunities no longer stretching

far as the sky is blue but stuck up
so many one-way streets. Are there clerks
still writing copperplate in a meticulous

slow hand, are there islands where no man
has ever stepped? The world is too small
now, smaller still in these last years,

what is inside has been piling up,
silting the drains. I don't have a new
overlay to combat spiky virus cells

circulating like planets. Perhaps
I could put my fears in a cosy cottage
tin, the kind of cottage that does not

exist except in fairy tales, I could
squeeze it into the cavity wall insulation,
or fling it far out to the ocean

where there is always something
unfinished. This life is measured
without a ruler, heel to toe, or in cubits,

while the greedy clock still ticks.
I was always unsure of the correct
orbits, how close was too close?

On a far wall the sky is enclosed
by four small panes of glass, spotted
curtains flounce an indifferent fandango.

Tina Cole

What we Learn from Stones

A woman walking her garden
is wearing a pale blue dress,
not the blue a child crayons
over a family home but more lilac,
like hollyhocks that have been

clambering through their own death

all summer and are now bent down
like old women. She picks up stones,
inspects each one, spits to reveal
true colours then pockets it as afternoon

heat presses its dry weight.

Youths' explosive with freedom
are exchanging dares, hands cupping
matches, dipping into their private
sun. They have smashed windows

on the lake, the path wet with smithereens,

each is weighing out a fist of gravel,
vying to cast the first stone. Look in the mirror,
have we learned the wisdom of glass house
rules? I was the girl who filled pockets with white
pebbles, did not gather moss, found a way home.

Tina Cole

Why We Stopped

We didn't know why
we drew these shapes.
Whenever we sat down to talk,
our hands would come alive
and our index fingers started sketching
what looked like
interlocking ellipses, eyes, and crosses.
When we first noticed it,
this subliminal transfer seemed intriguing.
Later we understood its implications.
There was no way to censor
what was being exchanged.
Whatever their source,
the messages delivered themselves.
This made us stop.
It wasn't worth the risk.

Michał Choiński

Yaffle Team

The Wife's Lament
After John Burnside

She wills him back by staring out to sea. Though it's not the sea
that's taken him, but the pull of January
river water, half thick with ice. Him, a single soul
smoking on deck, wrapped in the coat that will drown him.

The young wife finds solace in old knitting patterns,
makes money sewing wedding dresses, curtains
for half the village, while they talk behind their hands
when her pram becomes full with another man's children.

She sees his face
even when she's sure he's gone.
He comes to her bed
with the other man in it.
Marriage vows still melting
on their tongues. Or else

she finds him in the kitchen pouring water in the pot,
brings her a cup while she watches the mist come down
from the crag, her children tucked up, three to a bed.

The sea is as far away now
as it will get. The West coast
a week in a boarding house,
the landlady judgemental
and mean. But the widow

stares from the dormer in a draughty attic,
sure she can see him in his black wool coat.
The same swagger, a fag in his hand.

Gill Lambert

Yaffle Team

Propagating a treasure trove

If he could, he would make a hoard
of himself – bones of hollow
newspaper rolls, tied up with thick string.
Blood cells of dust particles floating, suspended
in his plasma of light and space;
wrapped in a film of clear plastic.

His love of little things; an idiosyncrasy.
He would have his face composed
of the wizened skin of old fruit –
too divine to dispose of.
His hair is a bird's nest found
in a hedge and taken as treasure.
All matt and straw – too beautiful
to let rot away in solitude.
If he could, he would become
his own collection.

He would let the clock whir and wind –
take control, to nurture the beauty
of every blooming mould.
Blossoming blues,
greens and purple.
Sprouting and exploding – these tiny
nebulae nestling in the palm of a hand –
peaceful and plentiful.
Static and stagnant.
All completely his.

To reign as king, rejoicing
in his secret kingdom –

Yaffle Team

glory in the gore
of daily growth.

Lorna Faye Dunsire

Yaffle Team

Asking for it

There was an evening, leaving late from work,
I found myself in the middle of a dark,
      industrial wasteland.

Along the long, grey road of featureless
units, too blank to be mysterious,
      I could see no one

until I came upon a clustered crowd
of five or six, outside an underground
      motor mechanic's shop,

relaxing from their labour, while I'd been,
all day, pushing a mouse around a screen.
      As I approached, one stopped

me, pointing to a moon-faced lad in grease-
stained overalls, who pouted and burlesqued
      a flutter of eyebrows.

What do you think? – What? – Do you fancy him?
He says he wants to fuck you. A fixed grin
      turned rigid on my mouth,

turned sour on his. Time stopped. I stood my ground
and held my breath – desperately cast around
      for anyone to help.

And no one came and no one left, until
I summoned up the words to break the spell,
      saying, *Nah, he's not my type.*

Yaffle Team

Part of me knew it was a joke, while part
had left me sweating, with a thumping heart,
    and this to understand:

it wasn't wit or courage that had kept
me safe from harm. It was nothing, except
    like them, I was a man.

Mike Farren

Closing Day

We shuffle along like the dazed refugees
our leader made. We stop to look
at products we still want, repeat our mantra:
Only buy what you can fit in your car.
There'll be no deliveries from tomorrow.
We let children pretend it will all be okay.
They play with cuddly toys in staged bedrooms
and we try to hide what our faces betray.

We love the poetry of these proper nouns:
Kallax, Klept, Empak, Ransare, Finskuren.
Some of us mouth the words as we move along.
We want to make a note of warehouse locations
but all the little pencils have gone.

When we've picked up what we need
we'll all get fed if we're prepared to queue;
they never run out of hot dogs here.
But some of us crave quarter pounders and lattes;
MacDonald's and Starbucks are pulling out too.

Mark Connors

You Knit

You eyed up my ply, colour, weight,
decided I would do, picked up your needle,
started to cast on with firm tension,

set a baseline on which to build
your pattern of behaviour –
a regular in and out,

with your own peculiar rhythm,
purl and plain, into the front
into the back,

until you got bored,
felt hemmed in, you said,
needed more variety.

You started to slip me one
sometimes, pulling the yarn
over my eyes, passing me over.

I knew you were dropping hints, stitches,
was aware of being raglan-shaped,
gradually tailed-off to nothing.

You left me, cast aside, only to try
to pick me up again weeks later,
unsure how to rejoin the thread.

I knew we were finished,
we were not an item.
it had all been a front.

There would be no making up.

Sharon Larkin

Also published by YAFFLE Press

Fairground	Penny Sharman	£6.50
The Magpie's Box	Terry Simpson	£6.50
Tadaima	Gill Lambert	£9.00
Whirlagust	Various	£9.00
All of the Moons	Mike Farren	£6.50
Moonlight through the Velux Window	Adrian Salmon	£6.50
Wilderness of Skin	Kathleen Strafford	£9.00
Quotidian	Paul Waring	£6.50
Reel Bradford	Yaffle 5	£10.00
Optics	Mark Connors	£10.00
Only Blood	Pat Edwards	£6.50
Pandemonium	Keith Lander	£6.50
And the Stones Fell Open	Various	£10.00
An Insubstantial Universe	Various	£10.00
Small Havocs	Matt Nicholson	£10.00
Enchanter's Nightshade	Simon Currie	£10.00
Fiery Daughters	Lorna Faye Dunsire	£6.50
Bloody Amazing	Various	£10.00
Whirlagust II	Various	£10.00
Cloud Cuckoo Café	Linda Marshall	£10.00
Learning from the Body	Sue Butler	£6.50
Symmetry of Folklore	Donna Irving	£7.00
Frisk	Peter Spafford	£10.00
Forged	Tina Cole	£7.00
Hi-Viz	Ben Banyard	£10.00
After	Mark Connors	£10.00
Untanglement	Matt Nicholson	£10.00
A Small Goodbye at Dawn	Gill Lambert	£10.00
The Doll's Hospital	Jenny Robb	£10.00

Please go to https://www.yafflepress.co.uk/shop to purchase any of the above titles.